Let me introduce myself

Hello, my name is Seth Lovett. You may remember me from that sketch that time, that music video, or in the background of your favorite show/movie....but probably not.

I was raised in a small Oklahoma town in a family of concrete finishers and firemen. The plus side to this is I have a strong work ethic, the downside is its not so easy to admit your dream is to be an actor and be shoved off to theater school or a film program. So I didn't. I worked all types of construction for years at many different company's. I show up, work hard, and when it was time to move up....I quit. I knew these jobs were not going to make me happy so I never really committed.

Until a job running heavy equipment at the University of Oklahoma, I enjoyed this job more than any job to this point. Then the dreaded day came, I was offered a better position. I knew if I took the position then i would never leave. That is a big decision to make about the next thirty years and I needed help to make it. I went home and discussed with my wife what to do next. She asked "What do you want to do?" I just blurted out, "All I have ever wanted to do is act!" She (a very supporting, lovely woman) just said "Okay, then do that".

At this point I had not really pursued acting. Thats no big deal, right?

Starting Out (Background)

Acting is a funny thing because it is an art but most people don't seem to see it that way. Not everyone thinks they can paint a masterpiece, play and instrument, or sculpt but it seems everyone thinks they can act.

I'm here to tell you that it is not that easy, it looks that way because you are watching a professional. With that understanding I decided to work with an acting coach to make sure I even had the ability before quitting my job. I flew to Los Angeles and worked with a coach one on one for 7 days. He seemed impressed and told me that I must move to L.A.

That was all the validation I needed so me and my wife packed up to chase a dream.

I dont suggest doing this.

I, like so many others thought I would run off to L.A. and somehow things would just start happening, I would get auditions and land jobs. I understood it would take hard work and some time but I didn't understand the scope of that.

In Hollywood they say it takes 7-10 years to become an overnight success. Just take a look at anyone that your just noticing, go to imdb and you will see they have probably been at it for a lot longer than you realize.

So if it doesnt happen overnight then how do I survive? Well Unless you are blessed with unlimited funding the first thing you will want to do is begin to make money.

The easiest way to make money and be on set is to sign up for background work. Check out CentralCasting.com

They have sign up two days a week, twice on Monday and twice on Wed. Orientation is a few hours and they go over the do's and dont's of being onset as background (Do-be early, Dont-talk to an actor, director, or basically anyone above you).

Each registration at "Central" will end up with a line wrapping around the room and out the door. There are thousands of people signing up every week so the competition to just be in the background is extensive. The way you get a job with Central is by calling in a listening to a recording for a description of you, which can be vague (those jobs fill up fast) or unrealistically specific. (These may pay a hair more and you wont fit the description, ever) "Were looking for a white male in his thirties, who has three nipples and can juggle chainsaws" Calling in can take most of your time, seriously, and you dont want that so I would suggest a calling service. They charge around $70 a month. Their job is to find you work and call you. They will tell you what your working on, where it is, your role, and what time to be there. Often you will receive a call in the evening and have a call time early morning with an inconvenient location. Oh and You dont want to no show or be late too often or they will fire you, which is strange cause you pay them.

There are a few calling services to choose from. Extrasmanagement will take everyone and then some are a little more picky, like Jessicas a list or Joeys list . Not that you have to be a model but they want diversity so if they have nine brad Pitt looking guys, they may not need another. And yes, there are plenty of Brad Pitt looking fellows doing background.

Once you are on set you will learn quickly that most people dont like the background. This is nothing against you or what your trying to do but anyone can sign up so a lot of people wont actually be pursuing a career in acting so they have a dont care attitude, which is very annoying to a production that is trying to get a lot of work done as fast as possible, people complain, A LOT, and are generally lazy. Also people will steal crafty (snacks) from the complimentary crafty bar. Not take two or three to their seat, I mean grab handfuls to take home. These sort of things give background a very bad reputation and you will be lumped into that. I also think its fair to mention it is not quite like this in a smaller market.

The most important thing is to be professional and treat it like a job and with respect. Even though it gets frustrating after a while because you will want to be a more important role try to have fun. Remember it is a privilege to be on set in the first place. Most of the time you are fed pretty great and at least your not doing something you hate.

Head shots

By the way, the order that this book is written is not necessarily the order to do things in. Its actually quite the opposite and thats why I'm writing this. So you wont waste as much or have as hard a time as I did.

Okay so you have made your way on set and realize you want to do more than stand in the background and be treated like a lampshade, except more annoying, its time to self submit. Where to begin?

If no one has told you how important a head shot is, I'm telling you now. ITS IMPORTANT! If you had your cousin take a picture with your new iphone and you think it really captures your essence "I mean, what do they want? Its a picture of me!" Your going to have a bad time.

You will need to have professional head shots done by someone who does professional head shots. There are all types of photographers so find one that specializes in head shots...have I said head shots enough?

This is the very first impression someone will get of you and it is very easy to spot someone who is not professional or seem to be taking what they are doing seriously. it took me some time actually believe this and get a head shot that didn't scream amateur. It will make all the difference.

When you email an agent, send a mailer, or self submit for things online your head shot will be the first thing anyone looks at. Often it will be in the middle of dozens or hundreds of others. In order to not just be skimmed over then it needs to pop.

Have a few different head shots for different occasions. A serious head shot is more theatrical while smiling with teeth is more commercial so understand which to send when submitting to things.

A head shot can say things that you dont want and you will not realize it. Nor your mommy, daddy, significant other, or basically anyone who knows you. They will see you. They know your personality and your mannerisms so post it somewhere or have a friend take it and ask what others see when they look at your picture. For Example

I am considered good looking and when my friend took my head shot and asked others they said things like "guy who isn't funny and wont stop telling jokes" or "guy who girl he loves doesnt know he exists" even "nice guy serial killer".

I have to admit I was not expecting those reactions. It was either time for new head shots or submit for weird guy next door roles.

So know what your head shot says and figure out how to make it say what you want.

Also it needs to look like you. If you get called in from your head shot and its been photo shopped to the point your sparkling like a twilight vampire and you walk in looking like an extra from walking dead, Not only will you not get the job, a casting director or agent will be upset for wasting their time. Who they wanted to see is not who walked in the door.

Lastly, you need to know who you are. If your 4'5" heavyset with acne...you probably will not get the role of the beauty or handsome guy also if your a GQ model you may not get the nerdiest kid in school part.

A Reel
(how and why)

As important as the head shot is to get someone to take a second look at you, what are they going to see?
To really get some attention you need a reel. Lets be honest, anybody can go have a picture taken. We have all seen glamor shots in all their glory. But can you act?
Oh yeah? prove it.
A reel should not be more then a minute and honestly with how busy everyone is it may only be watched for a few seconds so you want to put your best foot forward.
The footage should always be of you and very little, if any, of another actor.
It is not a bad idea to have various different reels set up. One for each genre you are wanting to be noticed in. If you are submitting to a comedy and someone begins to watch your reel and they see you crying for twenty

seconds they will probably click it off and move on. The first scene should represent the genre you are submitting for. Where do you get footage if no one will give you a chance to act in anything? Start with student films. I know no one thinks they need to do this at first. "I'm here to be on TV and in movies. I'm not wasting my time with student films."
I have met a lot of people who get to Hollywood with this frame of mind and no resume to back it up. I was one of those people but after sending out my head shot to as many people as I possibly could I would only get one response (on the off chance I even got a response) "Where is your reel?"
Finally I realized I needed to do some student films.
Film schools use the same equipment as the big boys so it is a great way to get good looking footage. Most of these schools have a bulletin board that you could go tack your head shot to. Try to go in and speak to someone about having you on reserve when they need an actor.

Another way to get footage together is to do it yourself.

The cameras on cell phones are completely capable of getting some cool looking shots but you need to be a little clever here. By that i mean Dont film yourself doing a monologue from your favorite movie in front of your refrigerator. Instead, be resourceful.

Find a couple of people to help you out. Write a script of you arguing, begging, flirting...whatever. These scenes dont need to be full scenes, just a blip of the climax of the conversation, just your character showing some sort of emotion then cut to some other random scene.

Have one friend hold the camera and show the edge of another friends head so your seen talking to another actor. This will look like it was actually from some sort of production. Good or bad at least your doing something. If you have other things handy use them. Pick up a guitar and film your girlfriend leaving because all you care about is music if your a woman be the girlfriend. Lay a motorcycle over and come running to your brother/father/boyfriends rescue. You get the gist of what to do here?

Remember we only need a few moments with your character not a full scene.

This part may or may not be possible but if you can get someone with a microphone to record sound for you, like a rhode Mic or a camera with a bullet Mic, these scenes will look a thousand times better.

Believe it or not people can tolerate a lower quality image but despise bad sound. You may see a great looking scene and not know exactly what it is thats making your skin crawl until you realize the sound quality if awful. Its the difference in home movie look and a "production"

If you cant do that still remember something is better than nothing. I wish someone told me to make my own reel in the very beginning. I think it would have helped me out exponentially.

Now as far as editing it together, there are a lot of inexpensive programs for simple video editing and if you have a mac book just use I movie. Hell the video editors on the android or Iphone are good enough to get the job done and even add music, text, and pictures. There is really NO excuse for you not to come up with some kind of footage.

After you book a job or two make a new reel and keep it up to date.

Resume

Your resume should be stapled to the back of your head shot. The paper in your printer is slightly bigger than your 8x10 head shot so be sure to trim the edges once its stapled to the back, trust me, you dont want to be that guy who has a white strip hanging over their picture.

As far as the layout, your name should be at the top with your or your agency contact info just below that. Under that should be your stats, which include your height, hair color, eye color, shirt size, jacket size, pant size, and dress size. Some people prefer to just have height, weight, hair, and eye color. This is fine as well but no one will scoff at more information about you and as a bonus, more stats means you can fill the page a little bit more if you dont have a ton to put on there and if you are reading this I'm assuming you dont.

After the stats comes your experience broken into sections (Theater, Film, Television, Commercial, Print or Editorial, Training, and Special Skills). Notice I did not put background, extra, or featured as a sections. Thats because it should not be on your resume if you are seeking representation in Hollywood.

You may not have any of the different sections I named with the exception of special skills. This is fine and fill that section up. Can you ride a bike? Swim? Play baseball? Play an instrument? Speak a second language? Ski?....et cetera. Put anything your good at or even mildly proficient. You may think anyone can do the things you can but trust me not everyone can. Not everyones environment allows them the same opportunities to do the same things growing up. When your adding another section it should be set up with three parts, the title, the role, the director/theater/photographer/studio. Training will be what you trained and where.

For example

Film
I want to act Lead Dir. Life

Television
Restless days Guest star ABC

Training
Cold reads Act camp

Special Skills
Just, a, ton, of different, thing, go, down, here, and, as, you, need, space, you, can, remove, some, of, the, less, impressive, skills,

Notice that I didn't put the name of the character. This is because unless your certain everyone has seen it or knows who it is then we wont really know the size of the role so use words like lead, guest star, and supporting. If you put Jim-bob as the role and I haven't seen RootinTootin boot Skootin then I'm not sure if your the lead or the bartender who had one line.

In theater however you could say you played Juliet if the production is Romeo and Juliet because everyone knows that role.

I'm aware that you also may not have any experience or anything to put down but you can remedy that.
But how? you may ask.
Start taking classes. A lot of people think they were just born to act, they are naturals. I'm telling you that all the best actors train with coaches.
This also does three very important things

NO 1. It will hone your skills making you more confident in a scene or audition because you know what you can do
NO 2. It gives you something to put on your resume. You can take a ton of different type of acting classes and start filling up space.
NO 3. And probably the most important thing it does is show whoever is reading your resume that even though you haven't been in anything you ARE serious. You are willing to spend your time and money to become a better actor, the actor they want.

Self Submitting

Now that you have your head shot, reel, and resume (because I'm certain you ran out and did each bit of advice as you read it without reading ahead), its time to land you some roles.

The best thing for you to do is sign up for the top two casting websites. These are the same websites used by everyone from the big agents to...well you. Agents of course get access to castings that you will not be able to because someone like NIKE doesnt want everyone with a computer submitting to their commercial.

The top dog in L.A. and N.Y. is probably CastingNetworks.com under which you have Lacasting.com and Nycasting.com. Sign up is fairly inexpensive at $25 dollars a year and free if you have an agent. The first picture is also free but it will be a $15 dollar charge for each additional picture. Sign up for photos unlimited and it is a $6 a month charge to

change your picture as often as you want.
For $5 dollars a month you can have digital hosting. Aka, your reel. You dont necessarily need to change your picture all the time but absolutely put your reel up there. When casting a project and a thousand different people submit one of the first things someone will do is filter the submissions by who has a reel and who doesnt so without it you may not even be seen.

When it comes to your resume its a pretty simple step by step and its free to change as often as you need to.

Time to begin searching for roles that you are a perfect fit for....well a good fit...okay, somehow fit. There will be a ton and new ones every day. Each submission is $0.99. Unless you sign up for Casting Billboard Unlimited which is $9.95 a month. I would highly suggest this because I promise you will find more than 10 submissions a month, probably in one day, that you want to submit for.

Dont submit for roles that dont fit you at least somewhat. If its asking for a petite Jessica Simpson type blond and you happen to be a heavyset Latina girl, dont submit for that. Or an athletic, ripped, Brad Pitt in fight club type and you have never worked out before. Dont submit for that.

It is a waste of everyones time and annoying to a casting director. I have sat on the other side of the table and helped cast an independent film. I can assure your there are hundreds or thousands of submissions for each role and it is anyone to already be overwhelmed with people and see someone and think "WTF are they submitting for this role for"

Also choose one role and submit, two max, and again fit the role or both. I saw the same wrong people submit for every role. This was a sure fire way to not be called in.

The next sight is ActorsAccess.com. This one is huge and nation wide. Though it is broken up into regions, not city or state. For example if you live in Oklahoma you will be in the Texas-south central region. There are only 12 regions, two of which are actually in Canada. So each region covers a pretty large area. Knowing this dont submit for anything you are not willing to travel to. Some people will allow video submissions but if you get the part you will still have to travel to play the role. If it is a small budget they will look for 'Local Hire' meaning someone who lives in close proximity. Not that they would not be willing to cast you, it really means they are not paying for your lodging while you are there.

This website is a lot like the other with a little different pricing. Sign up is free. You get 2 free pictures you can change anytime you want and any additional picture is $10. Your reel is a one time fee of $22 dollars a minute. Submissions are $2 per submission with picture only and $3 per submission with a reel. The submission fee can be avoided by joining their sister company showfax.com for $68 dollars a year.

A cool bonus is Showfax.com has a huge list of current scripts if you would like to study and familiarize yourself with how to read a screenplay.

A side note. Every job I booked in L.A. I was told that over a thousand people submitted from which they narrow down to a small percentage to actually come audition and ultimately landed on me. I couldn't believe that many people submit until I sat in the casting directors chair for a non paying short film and I assure you we had every bit that many people submit because everyone is wanting experience, footage, and just to act. In a smaller market however it may be more like 4 to 5 hundred. Either way competition is fierce and you will need to stay diligent with submitting every day.

Auditions

Holy crap! you got an audition? Seriously? Awesome!

Things just got real. An audition is the most nerve racking thing you will do in your life. Your dream feels like its on the line. You are shaking from adrenaline, fear, and excitement with no idea what to expect.

The number one fear in the world is public speaking, not only are you going to be speaking in front of strangers, you will be pretending to get emotional, talking to imaginary characters, reenacting a story someone else made up in their head. But this is what you wanted. This is what you have been working towards so let me give you a little advice about what to expect in an audition.

Firstly be early but not too early. Your call time is when it is for a reason. If you are going out for the parent and show up 40 minutes early and they are auditioning children you will only be in the way and left waiting. You can arrive 40 minutes early if you want to be safe, Make sure you know exactly where it is you have to be, find parking, and go over your character for a bit before actually going into the waiting room.

The waiting room itself can be a bit tense. Once you are signed in you may take a look around and start comparing yourself to everyone else there. "Man that guys in amazing shape. That guy over there looks like he has been doing this for a while. I'm pretty sure everyone here is better suited and more confident than me right now." DO NOT get into your own head, there is a reason you are there. The casting director has brought you in for one reason or another. I guarantee you they do not have the time to have people come in for just the experience.

Here is a secret to remember and give you some confidence. They want you to nail it. They want you to be the actor they have been searching for. That means they have done a good job finding the right people to audition and ultimately be cast. Now they can move to the next stage of production.

 Auditions are also very short. On average you will be in the room four minutes so be prepared. When you walk in the room. There will usually be two to three people that you will be auditioning for. You should walk in and have your head shot in hand. They need them less and less these days but its better to be prepared.

If they dont want it just set it down and pick it back up on your way out. You will be directed to your mark, a piece of tape on the floor, and ask you to slate your name for the camera. Sometimes they take pictures or ask you to turn to the left and the right for your profile. Normally the CD (casting director) will go over the scene shortly and then its your time to shine.

If you are given lines before hand it is best to be fully memorized. Some people like to have the paper in hand as a "just in case" or because they think it shows the director that this is just a rough draft of what you can do. I say you need to give 100% of what you can do at every audition. If you dont do it someone else will. If you go in and give 90% no one knows your doing this but you. You will just look like a bad actor because its presumed you are giving it everything you have. When you read a script you read it and you make decisions on how your character is behaving in the scene. They are getting nervous here so ill add a little voice crack, this spot they start to get angry better bring it up a notch, and here is the remorse so it will be spoken quieter with some pause.

No matter the decisions you make, make them with confidence.

If the scene is at a bar looking for the opposite sex and you decide you should cry for some strange reason. Then do it, but do it all the way. Otherwise you look like that bad actor again. If you make the wrong decision it is fine as long as you do it with conviction. The casting director knows what the director, writer, or producer wants out of the scene so they will direct you to go again. You will be given some direction "that was great, lets go again but this time maybe dont cry. Actually lets laugh in that moment"
It is very important to be able to take the direction of the casting director. You may have nailed the scene on the head the first time out but sometimes they say this time funny, this time angry, this time sad. Dont be discouraged or think you didn't do well or get hung up thinking you made the wrong decision. They may just be seeing if you can take direction. A lot of people will do a scene one way over and over and over until they couldn't do it another way if they had to. The CD asks the actor to do it with another emotion and the actor gives the same thing over and over. Even if you did great, they want to cast someone who can take the direction given and apply it.

Sometime you will not be given the script until you arrive at the casting office. This is called a cold read.

This is even a little more nerve racking. You have to memorize the lines, make decisions about the scene, and you will almost undoubtedly flub a line when your in there.

Its not a bad idea to practice at home with a couple of pages at a time of scripts off line. Like anything else the more you practice the better you will get. Choose a scene, look at it for ten minutes then film yourself a couple of time and then move on to another scene, and another, and another.

Then you have the improv audition. Probably the most nerve racking type of audition you will have. You are given some information about the scene, your character, and no lines. So you have to be great at thinking on your feet and just winging it. These can also be really fun once you become comfortable with them. You can actually say what you feel instead of lines off a page you would never say in your day to day life.

Often you do these scenes with another actor. Here is where it gets tricky. If you are not on the same page mentally it can be a disaster. Each of you will be making a mental picture of how you see the scene going.

If you are not in the ballpark of one another's vision then every line said by each actor will throw everything out of whack. You need to be quick to change your mental picture and just go wherever the scene takes you. Dont try to control whats happening or you will not be entertaining. A casting director told me "you want to act, it doesnt matter if you get the part. The audition is your chance to act! Be the character in the scene and most importantly have fun." Once the audition is over say thank you and leave. It is natural to want some sort of confirmation that you did well but dont stand there waiting for it. It can get pretty awkward for everyone. You dont want that feeling associated with your name or face. You want to be charming and fun. You want to be someone the CD would want to have lunch with and see again in the future. Make your impression and leave, dont hesitate unless they ask you to stay.

Finally there is an Eco cast or online casting in which you get to film your audition at home. This is great because you can do it as many times as you need and you save gas. Its not so great because you dont get to meet and have that real interaction.

No more direction so the decisions you make are set in stone. There is no one there to say lets try that scene this way.

Whatever the case, have fun, it really is fun, and I wish you the best of luck.

On Set

You landed a role. I always believed in you by the way.

When you get to set be early (just make that a habit, being early) and ready to go. People will treat the "Talent" like you are special but dont let that go to your head and be polite to everyone on set. Each person is as important as the next and people will remember who was kind and who wasn't. Being rude could make you lose a job in the future and being kind could be the reason you are called in for another project. Maybe the PA (production assistant) is wanting to be a big time director and he enjoyed your personality on set so he gives you a call to be a part of his independent film next month.

This is an industry of networking.

Once you find your way around and get settled the PA will give you some paperwork to fill out.

Tax papers and usually a non-disclosure agreement so that you will not be taking pictures or video of whats happening on set. This is very important to a production. If you are posting the plot of a series finale on social media they may have to rewrite and change direction. That would be very expensive and time consuming for production. Oh and you will be fired so theres that.

Always stay available. If you are leaving set for any reason let someone know where you can be found so there is no time wasted tracking you down.

When your in a scene dont call cut, this should go without saying but you would be surprised. That is the directors job. Also do not drop character until you here that word. The director may like whats happening in the scene and wants to see where it goes.

Dont ask to do your scene over and over. You may ask once but thats about it. The director was watching the scene and if he was not happy for any reason he would ask you to do it again. If they are "moving on" then they got what they wanted.

You did your job. You will probably wish there was more or you did something different but dont worry, you did great.

Every crew, production, and set is different so you will have to read each situation and act accordingly.

I think the most important thing to remember on set is that though this is fun it is still a job and requires you to remain professional.

Again have fun

Agencies

Look at you racking up all this experience. Your resume cant even contain all this stuff. That head shot looks great and your reel is exquisite. I'm sure you are growing out of self submitting and ready to find yourself an agent.

Lets be honest, you've been looking already. Haven't you?

There is no sure fire way to land an agency except persistence. This requires a lot of research on your part. Start with Google. Search for legitimate talent agencies and begin. Go to website after website finding out how to submit, whether it be on line or sending in a hard copy.

Write down names and addresses of all that will only accept hard copies so you will have an organized list. This should make it easier to send out multiples of your head shot, resume, and a dvd reel. If the agency will accept an online submission, dont waste time, do it right then and there. Submitting is something you could be doing for days and you may not hear anything back....at all. In that case. give up. ...Just kidding. You keep sending those emails and hard copies. I know the hard copies can get a bit expensive after buying everything you need as well as postage so with those I would wait a few months before resending.

Emails on the other hand are free so I would wait a month or two and try again. Keep going and searching until you get a call.

As I mentioned earlier this is a business of networking. When you are on set dont be afraid to talk about an agent. Its the best way to learn and possibly get a referral. I would not ask for a referral but if someone says they will vouch for you then that is great. Let them.

A lot of the agencies you find, especially the more legit and better known agencies will only take referral submissions so you can not submit to them any other way.

This is only a referral also, this does not mean you will get the call or the agent but it is one of the best ways to make that happen.

Once you do begin to get calls dont just run out and sign something out of desperation. You and the agent should be in sync with your goals. Have some questions prepared for them pertaining to what you want. If they are mainly runway and fashion but you but you want to be in film. They may not be the best fit for you. Do not be afraid to ask questions and have a dialouge. Find out as much as you can up from.

Most agencies have two year contracts. Some of these are exclusive (meaning you can not have another agent within so many miles). Or non-exclusive (have as many agents as you want).

If you are asked to sign an exclusive deal but are feeling unsure, ask for a trial. "This sounds good, I like everything so far but could you offer a 6 month trial. this way we can make certain that I work for you and you work for me so neither one of us is stuck in a contract we do not want to be in?!"

Most of the time they will say yes.

Be upfront with your agent about what you are willing to do and not do. If being in a sex scene is absolutely off the table be sure to bring that up or any other restrictions. If you are in a smaller market they may want you to travel. Possibly just for an audition. If this is something you cant do you need to make that known as well.

Your agent will be working hard finding you auditions and if they do not know these things up front then they will have wasted a lot of time and energy getting an audition for a role you dont want or can not make it to.

Also keep your agent in the know of your schedule. In the same sense if you are out of town for a few days or have conflicting work schedule, let your agent know not to book anything for you on those days.

Then there are the scammers. You will never pay an agency before you are with them. If you are told you need to get head shots through their photographer or a specific photographer, its a scam. They may tell you that you need new head shots and they may even have suggestions but if its a must then dont do it. The same goes for classes. "We are really interested in you but you are a little green, you need some runway training and on camera classes. Here are the classes we offer."

They are usually outrageous.
An agent will want you to continue training and your education but through an outside source of your choice. Usually much more affordable.
In short, an agency makes money when you make money. This is why it is so hard to be signed. Agencies are very picky. They need to think your going to do well, otherwise they are wasting time and not making money. As far as their fee. Agencies take between 10 and 20 percent of your earnings. For a union job you make a larger pay check and an agency can not legally take more than 10%. Non union however does not have any real legal restrictions or anyone fighting for you so they will take up to double for that.
This is where reading your contract is so important and finding all this out up front so you are not surprised when a chunk of change is missing.
But I say its better to have 80% of something than 100% of nothing.
Whether you are union or non I suggest finding an agent that is sag certified.
I hope this was helpful. I hope you have no problem finding an agency and have some ideas of what to look for when you do.
Happy hunting.

Unions

So your thinking its time to join the union. This is a tricky subject.
first of all you can't just call up SAG-AFTRA and say you want in. You need to qualify. If you are doing background qualifying can be difficult and take some time. You need to work three days as a union background member. This normally happens by total chance by way of a union member not showing up but production is required to have a certain number of union on set that day so they will pass along the paperwork to a non union member for the day. This is one of those moments where being really nice to the p.a. could pay off. You will need to hold on to the paperwork because you need proof of those three days. You may also get one if you are very unique and they need your particular look or skill in the background that day. This is pretty rare.
Another way is to have been a principle actor in a union project. This can be a new media, independent film, commercial...etc.
Once you have worked as a principal actor or your three days of background you enter

a 30 day Taft-Hartley period in which you can work union projects without being in the union. Once this thirty days is up you may ask for another 30 day extension after which point you become a must join. Meaning you can not work another union project without being a member. Another way to become eligible is to have been a member of a sister union for at least a year with at least one day paid as a principle actor in said union. These unions include ACTRA, AEA, AGMA, or AGVA.

Once you become eligible it is not free by any means. To join you will need to pay an upfront cost of $3000 as well as dues twice a year at a base rate of $201. If you have worked on many union projects you will also pay a percentage of your gross pay.

Being in the Union is a commitment. Once in the union you are no longer allowed to work on non-union projects so joining is not recommended until you have built up quite the resume. When the time comes that you feel you need to be in the union, talk it over with your agency first. They will guide you in what will be best for you. After all they dont make money unless you do and union money is better.

A smaller market, especially in a right to work state, it may be better to remain non-union for a while longer. I only say this because there is less union work so the experience will be harder to gain. If you are already in the union you can still audition for non-union roles but you can not work without a union contract. Some smaller productions may actually prefer this because it gives them a chance to make their project into a union project which in turn could benefit everyone involved. It is more prestigious to have worked on union projects. The unions also make sure you are paid fair and in a timely manner. Doing a non union job can take up to three months to be paid for. Union jobs, for the most part, are usually paid within thirty days.

Lets just say you want to work union any time you can.

So far I have been talking more in the sense that you would be a principal actor but what if you do a lot of background.

If you live in L.A. or N.Y. and you want to make a living being on set, it is nearly impossible to make enough without being in the union.

People argue that you work less being in the union but I would have to disagree. You may work less days a month but when you work you will make much more. This sounds like a win win to me. You are also treated better on set than you would be as a non union. The union makes sure of that and you are also taken a little more seriously. True you can not work non union but it does not take long as a union to never want to do non union background again. As far as more roles as a lead, keep auditioning. You have time since you are not constantly fighting for enough non union background work to survive. Keep fighting for projects to hire you and become union projects.

Also as a union member you can become a stand in on a union job. A stand in will come in between scenes and go through the actors movements and land on the actors marks so that the crew and d.p. can set up the lights and sound around him. This can take a while. Often on large sets walls come out, camera tacks and dollys go down, all types of production gear will have to be shifted.

While all this is going on the actor can take a

break or learn new lines.

This can be a regular 5 day a week job as a union member. You may make enough that you could survive for a while and concentrate solely on auditioning.

All in all I say build up an impressive resume and join if acting is your dream.

There will be a lot, lot, lot of talk on set concerning if the union is best for you. No one can make that decision but you. Remember misery loves company. Not everyone will be out for your best interests.

I wish I had a solid yes or no for you here but I just dont.

Trust yourself and make the best of it.

Conclusion

In conclusion. If you are living in a smaller market take the opportunity to learn as much as you can where you are. Take classes. Do short films. Do local commercials. Find you a local agent and work for them for a little while. Do everything you can do where you are before taking off. You will have an easier time getting that oh so important reel together outside of L.A. or N.Y. even if its just you doing it with a friend. A local pub may let you come in and film a scene after hours for free. Do not expect that to happen in the big markets.

Also acting is a job, one that you may not make much money at for quite some time. If you want to be an actor for a quick paycheck, your going to have a bad time. Acting needs to be something you love to do otherwise you will probably hate it. No matter where you are the place to start is a local acting class or coach. I promise you will not regret the experience and knowledge you will get from this.

I really hope this book was helpful to you and gave

you some direction. This was meant to give you an Idea of what to expect in the hopes you will get farther, faster. I want to encourage you to follow your dream. Do what makes you happy. Life is short so live yours by your rules. Never mind what society says you should do. Go, have experiences. Have fun. Make art. As Steve Martin said "Be so good they can't ignore you."

Thank you for reading and good night.

www.ingramcontent.com/pod-product-compliance
Lightning Source LLC
Chambersburg PA
CBHW071018180526
45168CB00003B/1466